Whiskers

Animals' Super Sensors

by Catherine Daly-Weir

illustrations by Tom Leonard

Random House 🏠 New York

It is night.

A cat is hunting a mouse
in a field of tall grass.

The cat cannot see the mouse.
But he knows where it is.
His whiskers feel the grass
move when the mouse runs by.

MEOW!

The cat pounces.

But the mouse slips

into a tiny hole.

That was a close one!

The mouse is safe—for now.

How did the mouse know
she could fit into the hole?

Her whiskers told her!
If her whiskers can fit,
so can the rest of her body.

Whiskers are special
hairs that can feel.
They are part of an
animal's sense of touch.

Have you ever played
pin-the-tail-on-the-donkey?
With a blindfold on,
you can't see anything.
So you use your hands
to feel the way.
That's a lot like the way
an animal uses its whiskers!

Naked mole rats live
in underground tunnels.
They are nearly blind.
But they never get lost.

The whiskers on their
heads and backs
help them feel
which way to go.

These seals swim
under the ice,
where the water is dark.
Their whiskers help them
find holes in the ice
so they can poke out
their heads to breathe.

A seal's whiskers
are also used for hunting.
The whiskers feel
ripples in the water
when a fish swims by.
Then it's dinnertime!

17

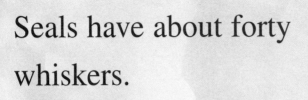

Seals have about forty
whiskers.
Walruses have almost 700!
That's more than
any other mammal.

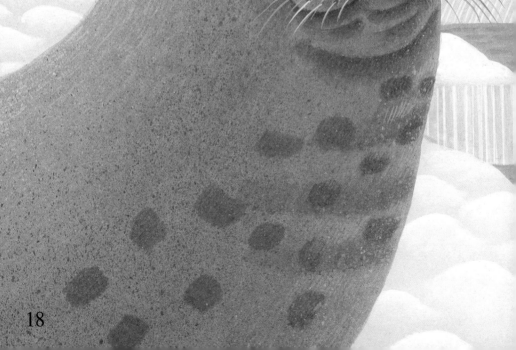

19

Walruses have very
sensitive whiskers.
They use them to find
clams and other food
on the ocean floor.
Their whiskers work
a lot like hands.

Walruses also use
their whiskers
to show affection.

A mother walrus will often
brush her whiskers
against her baby.

Have you ever seen a sea lion
balance a ball on his nose?
He was using his whiskers!

The sea lion's whiskers feel
which way the ball is going.
That way, the sea lion knows
which way to move his neck
so the ball won't fall off.

There are some people
who believe that whiskers
have special powers.
They think that
a tiger's whiskers
can cure toothaches,
or give people courage.

26

27

Some "whiskers" are not
really whiskers at all!

The *barbels* on this catfish
are made of skin, not hair.

This porcupine cannot
feel anything with his quills.

Whiskers come in all
shapes and sizes,
and animals use them
in different ways.